OTHER BOOKS BY MARVIN BELL

Nightworks: Poems 1962–2000 [2000]
Poetry for a Midsummer's Night [1998]
Wednesday: Selected Poems 1966–1997 [1998, Europe]
Ardor: The Book of the Dead Man, Vol. 2 [1997]
The Book of the Dead Man [1994]
A Marvin Bell Reader: Selected Poetry and Prose [1994]
Iris of Creation [1990]
New and Selected Poems [1987]
Drawn by Stones, by Earth, by Things That Have Been in the Fire [1984]
Old Snow Just Melting: Essays and Interviews [1983]
Segues: A Correspondence in Poetry (with William Stafford) [1983]
These Green-Going-to-Yellow [1981]
Stars Which See, Stars Which Do Not See [1977]
Residue of Song [1974]
The Escape into You [1971]
A Probable Volume of Dreams [1969]
Things We Dreamt We Died For [1966]

MARVIN BELL
RAMPANT
(POEMS)

COPPER CANYON PRESS

Cover art: Carl Morris, *Untitled (251)*, 1973. Reproduced by permission of Laura Russo Gallery.

Copper Canyon Press is in residence under the auspices of the Centrum Foundation at Fort Worden State Park in Port Townsend, Washington. Centrum sponsors artist residencies, education workshops for Washington State students and teachers, Blues, Jazz, and Fiddle Tunes festivals, classical music performances, and the Port Townsend Writers' Conference.

LIBRARY OF CONGRESS CATALOGING-IN-PUBLICATION DATA

Bell, Marvin.
  Rampant : poems / Marvin Bell.
    p. cm.
  ISBN 1–55659–206–x (cloth edition : alk. paper)
  I. Title.
PS3552.E52R36 2004
813'.54—dc22

                                        2003022728

98765432
FIRST PRINTING

COPPER CANYON PRESS
Post Office Box 271
Port Townsend, Washington 98368
www.coppercanyonpress.org

ACKNOWLEDGMENTS

Grateful acknowledgment is made to the editors of the
following publications, in which a number of these
poems appeared previously, some in earlier versions:

The American Poetry Review: "Journal of the Posthumous
Present."

Ashes Poetica, West Wall Press: "Ashes Poetica."

Crazy Horse: "The Castle," "Portal," "Resolving the Cold,"
"The Troubling," and "Typesetting *The Odyssey*."

Field: "Ulysses, Too, Was Sometimes Down at Heart."

Five Points: "Louis Braille" and "Rampant."

The Forward: "A Lesson from the Corps."

The Great River Arts Institute Poet Laureate Project,
Golgonooza Press: "The Parabolic Curve of the Red
Stem of a Dandelion Gone to Seed."

Hunger Mountain: "The New World" and "Persistent
Memory."

The Kenyon Review: "Bright Lights of January" and
"Epithalamium."

Near East Review: "Ashes Poetica," "Future Talk," and "Paris,
Bastille Day 2002."

Poetry: "Exotica" [under the title "Sounds of the Resurrected
Dead Man's Footsteps #68"] and "A Sky."

Poetry Miscellany: "Catalog with Illustrations," "Eyelashes, Doorknob and Pen," "It's Who I Am," and "Pastiche."

Poets Against the War, Thunder's Mouth Press/Nation Books: "A Lesson from the Corps."

Shenandoah: "Around Us" and "Winter in Sitges."

Solo: "By All Accounts: A Drowning" and "Vaccination Day."

TriQuarterly: "Another Primer about the Flag," "Boys Walking," and "View."

The Virginia Quarterly Review: "The Bones Repeat Themselves from the Bottom Upward," "Catatonia," and "Meditation."

Washington Square: "Of a Student."

"Catalog with Illustrations" was scored for music by David Gompper and performed by John Muriello and Tim Stalter at the University of Northern Iowa, 9/11/02.

"Journal of the Posthumous Present" was commissioned by the Getty Research Institute to reflect the Institute's theme for 2001–2002, "Frames of Viewing: Perception, Experience, Judgment."

Dorothy

CONTENTS

2

I

In Beirut, at the Worst of It

In Beirut, at the worst of it,
four men in their twenties play Russian roulette.
They sit in a black, derelict sedan, discarded
in a no-man's-land awash in stone,
once the facades of buildings—now leaning
to host a meandering barricade.
The cheap revolver they handle is heavier than it was
an hour ago when they set out.
It looks worn, as if the safety may not hold
or one might pull a misfire at the worst moment.
They hand it around with figs and an apple.
They have nothing to lose
and each takes a bite of the apple in turn,
then quickly places the barrel to his temple
and pulls the trigger. After four clicks,
they discuss whether or not to continue.
A jeep goes by but doesn't care to stop.
They live in a world fingertips cannot touch.
Some fatigues are boredom. Much is withheld.
One of them grabs the revolver into the back seat
and spins the chamber. "My turn," he says.
He has woken from fever to find a cold hell.
There are burns behind the forehead that do not smoke.
While the talk continues, one of them from a napkin
makes a bird you can make the tail wave on.

Eyelashes, Doorknob and Pen

He who has no handhold will slide over the edge.
When the conflagration comes—you know, the Rapture.
They send forth the child who limps, or the one with a stutter.
I can be saved, but barely, by an eyelash.
First I have to take hold of the doorknob and pass through.
I believe the way out is through the open door, always have.
I believe it of time and space, of the cloister and the pen.
There but for an eyelash or a nod go you and I to damnation.
Peoples everywhere know how a pen can give or take life.
I believe in the open door, I believe the earth will meet the sun.
But he thinks it will be tomorrow, and I think the day after
      tomorrow.
That's a big difference when you don't know how long a day is.
I have not wanted a watchtower, a lighthouse or an overlook.
I am something of a miner who has turned off his headlamp.
To better see in the dark, if you can believe it.
Whoosh, he can feel his eyes knit and unknit in the coal black.
His spine quivers like a long quill, quite like it.
This child of true believers wants to go to heaven.
He doesn't want to go underground with a geezer.
He releases the doorknob and pockets his ready pen.
Then he blinks, and blinks again, his lashes sticky in the heat.

Nature Morte?

I was standing at the corner of Main Street
when the plane came in too low, droning
past the office towers and rattling its hinges
as it searched for a paved strip among the fields
where it might fold itself through the tiers
of atmosphere until the odds became one-to-one.
Some people thought a crash was coming
and still do. Others said Aristotle was wrong
and art doesn't imitate nature because
art stops the plane before we can tell
and hangs the cotton in the air that sought
the peace of landing. When I reached home,
there was one white egg out of its carton
sitting next to a glass of milk and an orange.
Through the window of our antiquated house,
the neighborhood shook a little, not wavering
in its resolution but distorted by the aged glass.

Specific to Oahu

Goofyfoot is through the tall grasses and down
to the Banzai Pipeline, portaging a surfboard.
I'm too fond of sugarcane and bamboo
as one loves balsa because it is lighter
than it looks. As the bamboo is more tuneful.
My friend says now all art is urban and so it is
that a countryside of flowers has migrated
to urban windowsills. Caesar died because
they couldn't fathom his irrigation system. Or
they were sick of war or they needed fame.
The usual reasons. Harder to be left-handed
or left-footed on the board the way the tube runs.
We forget how much of Rome was Roman.
The lava that ran for miles to kiss the sea
looks smooth but will rip your soles. We forget
how much of Greece was Greek, and Polynesia
is not a way station en route to the big city.
The wind has risen, the bellysurfers have docked,
and far out where the lost fathers perished
they are standing up on the water as it coils.

Boys Walking

Sudan, 1988

When the famine had spread as far as the shadow
of a partial eclipse,
the older boys began to walk. They
were joined by other boys related to them
by hunger, and they breathed
shallow steps into the distance, believing
in food because they had known once
enough to eat. The bigger boys cared for
the little ones because they had heard stories
of the parents who were now constellations
by which they set their course. Also,
they had heard of the trucks whose gear-grinding
dusty clamor meant cargoes of grain.
It was too late to wait for crops that had thirsted
to bloom and died, and soon the shadow
in which they hid from the heat
would slide over the horizon, leaving them
in the public glare. Who cared?
This was to be another of the infamous marches,
writ next to the retreat from Stalingrad,
the forced trek on Bataan, Mao's thousand miles,
Perry sliding to the pole, but written
out of history, consigned to quartermaster logs
and mortuary tables,
the food that didn't travel, and the bodies
found hundreds of miles from home.

Meditation

You have to place a chair in the middle of the room,
otherwise empty. White walls, fresh paint.
You have to keep your eyes open
any time you sit. One lantern on the windowsill
at your back, and a conjunction of beads
that reduce the wind to soft clicks. Also,
you throw upon the white walls
half a dozen earthworms that have risen
to the sidewalk during the rain. You do this
solely by the power of your inner eye.
Project, also, on the wall, one owl,
at times wise and penitential on a branch,
at others calculating the swoop to home
while a young rabbit drips from its talons.
The young man who did this had composed
a lengthy letter to the newspaper concerning
the nature of voluntary action. We saw him
in the sunlight go into his room over the street.
There was a second storm brewing over the lake.
Apart from one wooden chair, a lantern
and twenty strings of beads, the room was bare.

Deluge

That a single drop of rain might hold within it a mile,
a column in which the fog and wind may conspire
with vapor trails of jets adrift in the kettle of the sky
and radio waves sliced from a billion eternal samples,
and yet this bead be thought pure, sanitary and chaste
in the country of the ideal, even when in weather
forthwith it arrives profusely, millions of bulbs shattering,
a torrent of seed burrowing downward where they fall,
piercing through faith and fiction, down past sentiment,
past reason, down downward and down to the mother lode,
there joining that amorphous pool where genetic material
awaits some infinitesimal particle to wed till happenstance
shall bring the earth, sky, ocean and sun to bear—
that thinkers should think each droplet discrete
pitches me into the infinite dark of origins and organs,
and robs me of my liberty to think in circles
when as now I am wet through to my liquid bones.

The New World

Light hung back at the horizon
as the high sails of the fleet came into view,
the water streaming all ways from the edge
and a scent of algae and a whispering.
There is always whispering at the ditch
where the runoff nourishes weeds.
Here come the Greeks seeking proof
like an armada of medical interns in sheets
hurrying toward a levitating corpse.
Such is the tide of knowing that when it recedes
the shore convulses with hunger pangs.
Their vision of gods and goddesses
fermented in the sea, and now
they have come from towers and fields
to make sense of the mythologies.
Their approaching sails wash the very white
from the air where Poseidon rises to bathe.
The gods do not cry much, even
for old men who know their days are few.
It is not for me to say how many years
it takes to reach the New World,
but something is in the air other than
the increased ozone that makes the sailors
look for cyclones and waterspouts.
Two young boys have untied a crab boat
and set out for the horizon, convinced
the whitecaps are part of their future.

Winter in Sitges

The old man building a boat on the beach
shows his son the right curve of a slat
to steer the sea past, and they plane
every day a board. Gaudí's structures
up the road trace a Catalonian warp
that wraps the air without enclosing it.
His cathedral remains unfinished but
people talk about it. I like to watch the boat
growing from the sand in the midst of
the Scandinavians in their bikinis
and the Spaniards in coats and scarves
smoking at the railing of the pier,
discussing what makes beauty tick.
The old man builds one boat a season,
all identical, every one seaworthy.
The blond girls rush the water in pairs
and don't look back. Nobody wears
a watch, and the sun travels only
a few stops on the sundial. The boat,
done, will be time-tight and watertight,
built to make shapes in the waves.

Of a Student

A lit cigarette is building an ash column
in the hand of the ethics teacher,
a contortionist in a classroom chair asking
if we can find a path from means to ends.
I can see the teleological seesaw quivering
but never mind. Up at the apartment
we have a pet mouse housed in glass bricks.
It has been snowing for weeks.
I hold my hands over my ears when I walk
at night when no one else is out. I
have been doing this for years and others
will tell me later it was only my footprints
there and back. The flowerpot on the sill
glows with a silky black calm and the cactus
pulls itself up its spine as if assured of sun.
We wait for the ash to fall but of course
he never lets it happen on its own.
Which is the happy light, dawn or dusk?
I can't think in the apartment, it's full,
so I leave again and again, tracking
across the bridge and up the hill,
and down the hill and across the bridge,
my ears frosted and my breath lit
in air now too brittle to reach zero.

The Troubling

I still think of the suicide standing on a ladder
to climb over a fence at the ball field
when he could have just walked around it.
He had a dark color for a last name
and seemed okay except for his father,
famous for a series of fire hazards
he made with his own hands and rented.
I must have let the book fall closed on which
the confession appeared after a candle
was applied. I dozed off without consigning
the name to memory and woke trying
to manufacture distance to go with time.
A white, slightly ruffled sky in late summer
covers time and the sun, and in any case
it isn't true what they say about the water
and the air and even the fire,
but about dirt what we heard was
ashes to ashes and dust to dust,
though we were not to recognize the voice.
There is a windowsill on which a frail
winged corpse of no weight has fallen
next to the husk of a ladybug.
There is an outside beyond the farthest
thing we can imagine. There is a schoolyard
with a fence around it to keep out bad ideas
just up the street from the bus station.

By All Accounts: A Drowning

Lamps running the riverbank draw a bead
on the bridge where the kid went
whirlpooling or undertowing
below the chilly mirror, dropping toward
his face rising from the bottom, meeting spring
head-on and feet first, finding a door where
no door is hung. Above his last scene
a plaque etches his loss into the psyche
of a figure standing above the water
watching the life force that commands
the daredevil and the hero, ready to volunteer
to tote the power of the sun past dusk
and wake on the other side of the river,
coming ashore to a thousand bouquets
forever damp, fresh and posthumous.

Amsterdam, the Dam

Milk-spills, guitars, drums and some smoke.
One could fashion a labyrinth from the roundabouts
of the new bodies of loose youngsters sprung
from trains and books of the sixties. It will take a week's
importation of batteries to keep all the headphones
whispering, and it's hard to be a sunflower
in canal weather. I'd go back myself
if there were enough fewer of the good things
so one might feel edgy on the outside. The universe
has expanded. The old rebellions are passé.
The gold Mozart still on his pedestal waved
when he saw us looking from next door—
while no one could see. The didgeridoo player
never took a breath. The man who danced as two
sailors knew things upside down and backward.
The obligatory pigeon man sold seed,
and this day a mariachi band wore colors
as bright as the missing sun. It's a kick to make
your own weather, says the backpack hurrying
to the cash machine. This is the life
they'll remember when the canal backs up,
the officials crack down on being young,
and the didgeridoo player sneaks a breath.

The Castle

There is a house being moved uphill.
They start again and again.
There are trumpets attacking, and drums
hammering the approach. There are jesters
and a man who runs ahead and kneels
to do close-up magic. Maybe it's just late
and I have gone into the past by slumping
into a doze over these Prague rooftops.
When I wake, the castle is still lit
beyond a forest studded with statuary.
The next afternoon we hike up to see
the watery curves of stone lovers
and the high chins and boots of poets.
The castle is hidden from us by brush,
but I can hear the fanfares and the wheels
as they push it higher up the hill
toward a later time, the last moments,
the last picture in the mind
of the child holding its mother's hand
as they run from the tanks.
When I wake again, the castle is dark.

Paris, Bastille Day 2002

Let's film it wherever there is venom
oozing from the trees. Art is cruel.
Let's train a camera on a length of string
signaling from a tree limb in the breeze.
We'll have an egg in a swinging birdcage.
Someone lifting weights in his underwear.
A girl smearing her lipstick on the face
in her mirror. Shadows on a window shade,
a large key, a Berber carpet, and let's
slit an eye again, art is cruel. This is only
the treatment, understand, a brainstorm,
a flight at harvest time through the dust
of haying, a slog through a gluey field
after the deluge, a shadowy figure
at the loft window above the parade.
The fireboats have reached their stations
on the Seine, afloat where the view
commands the fireworks. There's a swirl
in the air, mixing city and countryside.
There's a national gasp when the first
red rockets slice into the night sky.
It was on a holiday that fevers the city
when a madman took a shot at Chirac.
Bastille Day 2002, a gunman who wished
to be more than one of the crowd.
Art is cruel, calamity is routine, so let's
freeze it when Chirac's in his crosshairs.
We'll include a snapshot of the shooter
but distort it a bit for art's sake.

Louis Braille

The disinterment of Louis Braille carried out
on his one hundredth birthday so as
to install his corpse in the Pantheon was
as engaging a spectacle as any blind mouse jumping ship
could hope to encounter, intentions being
awkwardly good hearts for the one who
took military night-writing from its use in the dark
to communicate orders to the temporarily blind
where a match might draw sniper fire,
moved it into the light for the truly blind to see,
six dots being all he needed, thus
proving once again
that someone is always aiming higher.

Braille will go the way of Morse code,
abandoned to voice
responding to voice, things themselves thinking
as Norbert Wiener foresaw
at the dawn of cybernetics, before the movies knew,
and "smart" bombs, well before the end of humankind,
whose products will live on into eternity
mesmerizing the parasites that live in light,
thus granting to the mute
a last special rank and privilege so that
it will be impossible to say who cannot
speak and who has chosen
not to.

Vaccination Day

A cracking splintering the air above
the dormant grass leads back to a cardinal
knocking the frozen bath with its beak,
just as the sirens sound their monthly
tryout, reminding consumers to revisit
their survival gear, which now includes
agents and anti-agents, the usual tools,
dry food, and of course plenty of water.
Cables at treeline shiver with the latest
alert, and the faces of the wanted are dealt
across a plane of video monitors like
a deck of collectible playing cards.
It will soon be vaccination day, to go with
a lengthening string of memorial days
for those who once practiced fire drills.
Survival favors those who can find water
in ice, and the redbird ratchets up
the pace of his pickax, his head affirming
the effort it takes to break through.

A Lesson from the Corps

When you find the body, it has cauliflower ears.
It stinks of dead worms, the blood crumbles between
    your fingers.
When you find the body, the sleeves of the combat fatigues are
    in shreds.
Its face is puce, its torso black and blue, its guts purple, but the
    teeth still gleam, and the bones will shine up when cleaned.
Your saliva congeals, you taste dried paste.
Later, you may feel shame for noticing the colors or hating
    the smell.
You were schooled to do this.
To yank the dog tag off with a snap.
You were trained not to answer back to the silence.
There is a hiss as you compel the metal tag between the teeth.

This day may become a whiteout, a glare, a deficit in memory.
A place too barren even for a shriek.
A picture that didn't develop, just a clear negative.
For nothing recorded the thump of the bullet as it hit, or the
    webbing wet inside his helmet liner, or the echoing
    within the helmet itself.
But you may think you remember the shudder you didn't see
    when he died.
You may imagine the last word, the mouth before the
    lingering stare.
The machinery of his broken chest may appear in dreams.
You may see the eyes, and hear the last expulsion of air.
He is the vault now for your questions to God.
Only the dead can tell you the distance from here to there.

Future Talk

Germs, viruses and parasites
gathered in the classroom
to discuss the beginnings of
intelligent life. They discussed
the stupid dinosaurs, who,
they agreed, were dumber than
dirt and deserved to die out.
They recalled the passenger pigeon,
the whale, the owl, the wolf,
and, while they admired each
for something, none of these
apparently had the right stuff.
Then the talk turned to mankind,
and there was some disagreement
as to the meaning of "human."
There was the usual shaking
of heads, up and down, over
how easy it had been to overcome
the kind of man that mankind
had been, since it was
merely necessary to penetrate him
and then to mutate before
each new weapon: biological,
chemical or radiological. Of course,
these were the ultimate
biological weapons, and now they
smiled at the utter simplicity—
the naturalness—of it all.
Everyone said that mankind,

whatever it was, was certainly
unfit for lengthy survival,
and of course to say so was so
so obvious that the teacher
warned them against pride,
which they did not have or need.

Resolving the Cold

Sunshine greases the streets at thirty degrees
and the new aluminum gutters going up
the roof across the way, on this final day
of 2002 when resolution commands the sense
of a last chance. But for the grace of
a whisper deftly placed in the office
or the unforeseen storm that made the roof leak
one might have lived another life
otherwise employed. Seamless aluminum
should last a lifetime, if white overalls standing
on a red ladder can fix it for good and still
listen to the ball game. We have custody of
a house, a neighborhood, some years
when this or that needed repair. In December
the phone lines shimmer and the stripped
maples husband the summer deep down.
Tonight it's down to the dregs, who set foot
across the canyon of New Year's Eve.
Like water that has pooled in a depression
loosed to flow, laden as it may be
with leaf rot and sediment, the year returns
to ground zero and the numbers
begin again, as if we had as many tasks
as there are raindrops, each lodged in a vow
to start from fresh, intoxicated by youth.

Catalog with Illustrations

The beauty of an old desk blotter where ink stains grew into
    the shapes of ships in a turbulent ocean,
and the ticking of the clock in the sunlight thickened by dust.
The clacking of the typewriter keys, the big zipper sound of
    the carriage return,
and the sound of the struck bell muffled in the drapes.
The air was rich with time, when there was still time.
The letter ripened slowly in the typewriter.
The minute hand took a second to move one digit.
Under the glass that covered the desktop, a map and
    family photos.

A Sky

The sky had been burning for some time, and our eyes hurt.
This new burning sky came down in pieces.
It fell on every continent and into each of the seven seas.
It was not a fable or a rumor, it was actual pieces of our lives
    on Earth.
It could not be marketed, no demand for it could be mined.
The stock market quivered.
The meters of taxis began to spin.
People who usually rode, walked, and people who usually
    walked, hid.
The newspaper ran a three-line six-column headline.
Sputnik had gone up and come down long ago.
Hundreds of satellites since had burned through the
    atmosphere.
This day the morning dew ascended forever.
The sky cried dry tears that turned into grit-laden globes.
A million little earths came crashing to Earth.
This happened on the island of Manhattan and also England.
It took place over Asia in a time not so long ago.
It happened in the age of catapults.
It thickened in the age of artillery and spread in the age
    of bombers.
It came from right and left, from above and below.
The universal principle, it took place time and again.
Above the sky falling, there was always another sky.
People gathered in the streets to salute the new sky.
Children climbed on their parents' shoulders to touch it.
But the new sky was still out of reach, though it seemed lower.

Another Primer about the Flag

And what it means. Flags have been planted
at the poles, flags fly at half-mast,
and some flags are folded triangles
in a drawer. There's a flag on the card
a family puts in a window
when they have given a son or daughter
to the flag. I saw a man strumming a guitar,
wearing a flag hat, and there's a colonel
who sleeps on flag-imprinted bedsheets.
Many people twice a day stand to salute
in the direction of the flag. There are little flags
in the ground where they play taps. The crowd
at the game usually knows where the flag is.
People who sing "Dixie" have a flag. They
wave it like a shirt in a bullring.
If you want to carry the flag in front of
a parade, you must wear a special belt.
A flag is not a dishrag, though soldiers bring it
when they're mopping up. When you
pledge allegiance to the flag, you put one hand
over your heart, but when you salute
you hold your hand at your head like a visor. That's why
you don't have to salute in the rain. Oil on a racetrack
means a yellow flag. A big accident means red.
At the finish the winner's flag flutters overhead
like a melted chessboard. And you take a lap.
A white flag means surrender, but
sometimes it just means you gave up your shirt.

Around Us

We need some pines to assuage the darkness
when it blankets the mind,
we need a silvery stream that banks as smoothly
as a plane's wing, and a worn bed of
needles to pad the rumble that fills the mind,
and a blur or two of a wild thing
that sees and is not seen. We need these things
between appointments, after work,
and, if we keep them, then someone someday,
lying down after a walk
and supper, with the fire hole wet down,
the whole night sky set at a particular
time, without numbers or hours, will cause
a little sound of thanks—a zipper or a snap—
to close round the moment and the thought
of whatever good we did.

Exotica

1. Brain, Grain and Buckle

These rainfalls gossip of summer to the corn seeds and beans.
They whisper of orchids, of grain bracelets in the fields.
Who wears boots or galoshes now will wear slippers in
    two months.
And the corn erect a funhouse for the little ones.
First there are months of tools and tractors borne across
    the land.
And the wind slapping the barn door like a cheap cabinet.
Of this passage from hunger to plenty, the diminutive
    Aristotle said nothing.
That such a field of dreams could be sown in the corn belt.
See the blue that sucks up the thoughts of great cities.
Consider the dreams that roam the land without tongue.
And the happy children still fleeing through green passages.
Their world organic, their path among green banners.
Acres held by a belt with no buckle.

2. Bean, Sickle and Bucket

There will be no baseball in Circe's garden.
So precious is she that she dines on white beans and orchids.
And the caviar said to be salted with men's blood.
Metered passages of gossip enthralled the Greeks.
They heard in them the wind sickling the waves off Crete.
Hence, their poets drank wine by the bucket and sang to
    the gods.
They danced with their arms and shoulders.

They braced themselves in a boot-clad line for the climb up
    Parnassus.
While their eyes played the dance floor seeking shipmates.
They also loved the organdy of the open sea.
And yes there was grain in the liquor.
They were not of one mind only, they ate eel and octopus.
They had history in their thoughts, but they could dance.

Catatonia

In the country of Catatonia,
mourning doves attack a plastic owl.
A man shouldering an ax
hears a blade of grass cry, "Save me."
A noose dangling from a tree limb
turns itself inside out.
All the church crosses have been laid end to end
to form a track for a train.

The train hisses at inertia.
It wants to waken the hillside
and cause the ice to crack from the passes.
It has a will of iron
and has been used to transport prisoners
from Catatonia to Bermuda
where everyone is sunny and the children
wait all year to go to camp.

Ashes Poetica

Concerning a pair of shoes that stands beside the bed
in league with the night,
the consorts of sweat and the stone ends of toes,
the inaccessible spiders of rooms used only after dark
and the family of things that live between speaking and
    not speaking.
In the room, also, are a dead ear, a covered eye
and a stage trod upon by the shades of experienced actors.
A body lying crushed against the sheets, a pillow
imprisoning a head, medicinal flowers in dark water—
and then the corpse turns suddenly, so that the dead ear
comes alive, and the cover of the eye is revealed to be thin skin.
Corpuscles of light descend from darkness, randomly, quietly,
and are able to penetrate the exposed eye
where they fall into bits and pieces, trying to form a picture.
But it is not to be permitted, even when the shoes
stop breathing and grow cold, even though the spider
has gone deep into the corner to try to pull down the walls,
even though eyes watch which could not see in light—
no matter what, nothing is to be taken from sleep
unless it has been burned. And none are to be remembered
from among the players, even though they may attempt
memorable speeches and strike dramatic poses.
For such is the destitution of the body
that its destiny must be dispersed by any means necessary,
even if it means the day is to be accompanied

by the clamoring of a pestilent chorus from beneath a
        sunken sea,
and the night is to be swallowed by sackcloth
as the feet each day are swallowed by shoes,
and because of fate someone has had to invent fire.

Portal

He was given to see through time.
He made sense of near-autism and near-schizophrenia.
A door handle turned on its own, back and forth.
On the other side a blinding light.
Grainy apparitions rode the third rail beneath the sidewalk.
City is city.

Extravaganza: Dismal Water of the Swamp

This I know. As scientists who long to ride a beam of sunlight, the smallest ray, through the microscope, and by an act of empathy too tiny to interest that great circle of men who populate eternity with their complaints yet never see that which is in front of their faces, we, my companions and I, lacking the language for our feelings, every day arrived at one of the scruffy docks that clung to the end of each road that met the bay. Although we did not know it at the time, we would have fought for these oases, these collections of broken boards and old tires, these little peninsulas of junk precariously perched on rotted logs that revealed in low tide a calcified wrapping of sea creatures who lived and died at the whim of water and man. We were, after all, the scientists of our own lives, thrown out of the laboratories, dismissed from the schools, with predictions that we would never amount to anything. We were never to see, our teachers told us, what we had. And yet we arrived each afternoon at the last squares of streets named for bridges and bodies of water, ourselves so full of energy and so afraid of passion that, although we could never have fathomed why, the nearby reed-infested bogs of festering mud, which led nowhere, which were of no use to the town, which were, to the civic mind, neither water nor land—these captivated us, surrounded us as we sat in silence, occasionally tossing a pebble into the rushes or picking a blade of grass, hidden from duty by the swaying forest of the swamps. We who were to leave that place to the developers and vacationers, those who filled in the marshes and reclaimed the docks for appearances, who came for a weekend or a month, or built and sold out and went, and whose real lives would always be elsewhere—we who left the end of the road to others were unable to express the perfect solitude we shared and did not violate in those hours. Sometimes the rushes swept to and fro in the wind that accompanied a sea of whitecaps. The rougher the day, the more likely we were to linger. I suppose that we were at the end of something, though we did not know it. I know that we were in love and did not want it to end. We had been born to island life. And so there remains within me the landmarks, buoys and shoreline, the channels among sandbars, the walkways made of old lumber, by which we left the company of others and returned. I carry the memory of swamps that gave the lie to dead ends. When the wind pauses, I can hear a sputtering under the rushes, beneath the mud.

Rampant

His eyes have lodged in the mirror
two holes without backing
two marbles on a plain sea
without tides or whitecaps
two nothings on the razor edge
of reality
two archaic digs in a skull
one imagines
wore some sort of seeing aids
which slipped
down the bridge of his nose
so that he couldn't see himself
except by throwing his head back
at a strict angle
which caused his eyes
to roll back into his head
as if he spent nights
on his back
making shadows
through squinted eyes
with his hands
the way children do
in the dark
by the light of the moon
not knowing
what is out there.

He Sees Himself

He sees himself.
He can see the front of himself but not the back.
As if he were coming toward himself.
His jacket is open, his shirt clean but rumpled.
He looks as if he has just woken up.
It's not impossible that he has thoughts.
His eyes, his eyes.
He can't see the soul through his eyes.
Nor do they mirror it.
He can't see beauty in the eye of the beholder.
He sees himself approach but come no closer.
The sense of always arriving.
Do you recognize yourself in this portrait?
He is always awake in the other's dreams.
He knows a lot about me, this dreamer.
I watch him dream.
I see him start away from me only to meet himself.
Waking, I am twisted in the bedsheets.
Sunlight washes him out of my eye.
He must have been wearing a white shirt for work.
He sees himself in the window behind me.
He sees my back reflected in the glass.
As if I were moving away as I came closer.
He keeps his thoughts to himself.

Epithalamium

If you twist a rope
twist it and twist it
no matter how long a rope it is
after a while you cannot make one more turn
without skinning your palms
and burning the backs of your knuckles
and if you lift one hand from the rope
to get a better grip
the whole thing springs back
toward its most direct shape
its original being
with the fury of a coiled spring
at having been diverted from its purpose.
Every fiber of its being
rolls over on its back
the way molecules according to science
align themselves magnetically.
It is instructive to imagine that
the atoms in a rope
know where they belong
when you see those sad pieces of twine
that retail clerks wind around
boxes of socks and drinking glasses,
from which broken strands seem to reproduce
and under which the box strains outward.
And it is comforting to acknowledge it
when the molecules of a husband align themselves
with those of a wife

and the iron filings on the desk
connect the two ends of a horseshoe magnet underneath
as the moon follows the earth
forever in darkness.

The Parabolic Curve of the Red Stem of a Dandelion Gone to Seed

Anything tasting like moist straw is good now.
Then, I sat on the grass and waited for the dandelions
to spray their white feathers in the wind,
and a fly came by to see what had spoiled,
but nothing had. A sweat bee the size of my fingernail
worked nearby, taking what it needed.
The taste of whatever bloomed near common grass
is good now. Then, a bird hid in the pine,
biting off yells that seemed to say all seeds were his
by right. Then I noticed, for the first time, I believe,
the easy, fluent curve of their stems.
I was in love with the commonest weed of all,
more for the slim line of its stem
than for the expression of its face. O my secret,
scattered among the green leavings of time—
weren't we as resilient a pair as this straw in the wind,
and weren't our steps together as light
as the crackling of rice paper? I hear that crackling begin
again, as I split the stem of the dandelion,
and fold it and chew on it. Because then
the dandelion towered over its tiny estate, today
I reach down to pull one from the earth, recklessly,
and carry it awhile, and taste it and drop it.

Typesetting *The Odyssey*

Norton is smoking a pipe as he slots the letters
into a type stick, the California job case
thinning out as he uses up the *m*'s and *n*'s
and the *e*'s despite their number. It's a case of
how many individual acts can a man get right
in one hand, yes it's one more revision of thought
sweating into labor and a philosophy of acts
vis-à-vis the whole tenor of a life. That is,
shall a man be stoned to death by his neighbors,
or is it sufficient to have one representative
of all who are without sin take the rap. How
on this bumpy earth can a typesetter make all
the right draws in perfect order, not even one
upside-down italic *x*? He can't. The classics
are the place for the gods, aglitter in the ether,
flaming the sea with their haute-supreme
perfection, and sacrosanct on their home turf:
ageless luminaries of an age when the voyage
knocked you off your pins and Troy fell.

It's Who I Am

The smell of dead fish belly-up in the creek,
which slid from the bay all the way to Main,
thickened the summer till it lay on our arms
like the sky itself and our impenetrable future. Who
did we think we were? There are lamps on the cruiser
Doctor Jones keeps in a boathouse where we go to smoke,
and when someone comes we pop out of the hatches,
breaking the bulbs, which spew clouds of poison
so we can't close up and a cop guards the boathouse
a week while we ride bikes elsewhere down the quarry hill,
sand rasping our legs and the sun eating our backs.

That's the smell of home on my island—that green, fishy,
eggy, algal, slick-sliding silvery what's-in-the-mud air
that blanketed the days we spent dangling a pin on a string
and our faces freckling the green water. Who were we,
really? The big war has left aircraft-spotting stations
on the dock where we hole up to study plane silhouettes
on the wall, grit of sawdust in our mouths, scanning the sky,
while the flounder nibble in the deep and the weakfish
wait for dusk when hard-shell crabs will slice sideways into
our flashlights to be netted and boiled for dinner,
and an incoming tide wrap the clam boats at the pier.

The Bones Repeat Themselves from the Bottom Upward

It was not the time to be thinking of spring.
The boats were at their moorings,
applauding the good wood. The tires were hung
from the timbers and did not look fatigued
to be stationed for good at the pier. The weekend rowboats
had gone out and come in. During the day,
one could see from shore the oars held up to ask
for help, and the sea churning up light.
There is a fingerprint somewhere that will matter,
a bloodstain on an oarlock, a fright that will never
surface or yell out, because it will never be time to.
Later there will be a wedding in the leaves
by the white church where the Boy Scouts box
in the basement, trying to be brave.
The owner of the fishing station watches the sea
through binoculars, fixing on the darker water
where the boats clustered to thin a school.
The days have been growing raw,
and he is willing to give the last ones five minutes
before he rips the tide apart with an inboard
and drags to the beach those who didn't
see the end coming.

Ulysses, Too, Was Sometimes Down at Heart

The way it happens, we go way up,
then way down. Hormones soak us. A watery
solicitation insinuates, whispers, promises:
our tissues quiver for an hour or half a day.
Then the tide turns, and we touch bottom.
We didn't do, or forgot. There was a resolution
above us. High, out of reach. We have learned to
hear the sound of a rain cloud forming. A mast
nearly snaps. We make that promise again—
to be steadier, to spend the highs slowly. We picture
an even channel flowing between two rocks. Once,
we stood above them and could see forever. Later,
we escaped with our lives. Names for these rocks
were already known in the age of the classics.
We know because we founder. Become inert.
They were gods, once: Mania and Depression.
In a religious time. A time of voyages.

Persistent Memory

There was a twenty-four-hour greasy spoon,
now gone, but don't slow down.
There was a bookstore in which each book was a lost treasure,
now departed, but don't slow down.
And the brick church the old professor hammered his protocols
into the door of, our local Martin Luther,
don't slow down. The arts take over when churches go,
and come masseuses, martial arts, therapies
of waxes and rose hips, and posters of Noah's animals,
and they don't slow down.
And that massive mill in the window of the coffee shop
that burned alongside the bookstore,
when one with frozen pipes employed a blowtorch,
don't slow down. And the bar with the collection of clocks
not all lined up like today,
don't slow down. The garage full of dolls.
Nights, I can see shadows on the walls in the dark,
after lights-out with the shades drawn.
One stops to wonder.
I once photographed a boy on a trampoline
and now he's up in the air
and won't come down. And I took pictures of
cellophane, which is to say light, and of skin,
which is to say light, and nudes
shaped by one tinny lamp hung on the back
of a rocking chair, but the model
needed only the light
of one breast. I have a cold spot in my brain
where the light settled.

Bright Lights of January

An oak branch chewed down to the meat
and the window of a car grumbling over gravel
toward groceries and the news are midmorning's
bright lights of January. The brittle leaves pool
in depressions, tar and caulking constrict
and woodsmoke falls from the roofs. These
are the fallow days when opera retreats
backstage in costumes and scenery
between seasons. The café trade is thin.
Into this resonant cavity there comes a cable
singing of tropical seasons where the fish run
to be hooked and spring at the creel while
elsewhere the intolerable poverty continues
fresh and refreshed on a home monitor
the other side of need. The missionaries
killed for religious reasons keep going
for religious reasons, and their names too
are etched in downloads and town memorials
with all the other walls of names. The news
arrives with the groceries, where the one-eyed
man may be king but the gods are blind.

View

When you look through the window in Sag Harbor and see
    the trees, and you think they are blocking your view, you
    are looking, even then, at the water.
Those leaves are mainly water, the air between you and them
    mainly water.
The distance, as the bird flies or the squirrel scampers,
    mainly water.
You yourself are a kind of flooded hollow hull.
On the bays, on land that was water, on back roads that float
    in floodplains, you bob like a log separated from its boom.
And when the bodies fall from shrapnel or direct hits, they fall
    so far they begin to dissolve.
Interred as flesh, they become air, leaving a chart of bones.
You think you can't see the current war and don't want to, but
    the war is in the trees.
The leaves fall, and there it is.
The branches of the evergreen sway to one side, and you see it.
It is the ocean between us that makes others seem so far away.
In Sag Harbor, a slight seacoast breeze at forty degrees can
    shave your skin.
So people stay in their cars to sit by the docks.
It's a busy day when looking out to sea is the one thing one
    has to do in the dark before going home to sleep.
People who never travel otherwise think they can see England.
Not so much see it with their own two eyes as with their
    imaginations.
Their idea of Europe extends beyond their line of sight.
The morning papers will carry the battle reports.

The gossip from the front lines is that the enemy has
melted away.
We hear the eyes in the sky can find only civilians now.
We want justice, not just a momentary view of justice.
A black cloud has blocked the dawn.
We know it is morning by the dew and the frost on the
windowpanes.

Pastiche

Were we ever in Nîmes at the Temple of Diana?
Did the ancient tiles tell the story?
One goes forward to Volubilis, or goes on to Machu Picchu.
The narrow rails exist only to take us to the ruins.
The past is coming, wait and see.
That is what makes me happy with my eyes closed.
I have met a man who lives in Utopia, which is not a place.

2
Journal of the Posthumous Present

Journal of the Posthumous Present

Resonance pleases.
A leaking resonance, likewise, pleases.

1. Location of the Question:
Seurat's "L'Ile de la Grande Jatte"

He sat before the canvas and asked it, "What is beauty?"
As once he lay on his back to ask the oak, "What is a mind?"
He inquired of the paint, and of the palette behind it.
As once he questioned the oak and the wind threading
    its leaves.
He believed then that when a tree says hush it doesn't mean it.
He sensed that sensation in art was a penny-ante value.
The oak swept aside his words, and no answer could be
    detected.
Even if it was called for, if it was truly desired, if he couldn't
    live without it.
And the black that was not black but Seurat's black defied
    his eye.
His head above water in the wet air, and the tree throwing
    out lifelines.
Slap of leaf, scent of cut grass, time and a weed to chew on.
Wait, was he not by the river as others had been pictured
    by water?
In a mood to ape nature, not to copy but to imitate.
Nights, the leftover nostalgia of dusk smearing the horizon.
Mornings, a leftover moon in which to read the future.
Oh, I confuse myself with myself, now with then, and who
    spoke.

I imagine myself Seurat and try, and fail, to paint it as he did.

Natural when young to think the leaves whisper.

To suppose that the artists are helpless before the sublime.

Inevitable in youth to believe they tell you their secrets.

And the animals, what are they thinking, is it thought?

Ineffably, the deer stare into your soul before they spook.

The homely groundhog, hastening to cross, looks down in
     acknowledgment.

While a painting that hugs a century oozes with its lost past.

That to its maker was mote and color—timely, methodical.

A rage to do things others cannot, to make them see it
       your way.

So I too walked with my neck bent, looking at my shoes.

That is how I came to stay up late to see the moon pale.

The night as I write this is a shadow that will pass, is passing.

And the wild owls my pets, where are they tonight?

They do not question perception, they hunt in the dark.

Have they gone back in time to hoot at that boy I was?

Do they object to his spending his days talking to a tree?

In the belly of its shadow, his face aglow?

We always see something, the owls and I.

The deer at the roses, the fox in the headlights, the bats
     in distress.

His favorites were the oak and maple, but mine are the willow,
     the ash and the scruffy box elder.

He grew up is all, and saw that beauty is a sop to terror.

He saw like you that we are but do not know yet what it
     means to be.

Spring's profusion is blinding to wide eyes.

It was warm and wet, and the leaves dripped ink into his veins.

2. Of Salome: On Death and Beauty

I was not, in the beginning of time, a head on a plate.
I was a foot that wriggled and writhed to escape.
I curled my toes to kick the wall, and I carried the bruise.
I used my instep like the back of my hand.
That was then, in a protected shadow, which remains as it was.

The hand was the hand and the foot was the foot.
Elsewhere, the head and groin were interchangeable.
Tonight, I hold my life in my hands, and my hands are small.
What if I am asked to hand over my life in a week?
Tonight, in a week, a year, an hour—all the same afterward.

My head on a plate, and what will it bring at auction?
Salome liked it when I did what she said to.
Otherwise, we had what might be considered a falling out.
The guilt was not helpful and the condition inoperable.
I am tonight a pilgrim in a corridor of moonlight.

I, whose lot is the most one should ask, have learned a lesson.
I think of things formerly too terrible to contemplate.
And tell my friends, the fly and the spider.
The soup tastes like a sacrifice.
I have taken in my belt.

I weary of carrying my head in on a plate.
If I were allowed to drink and laugh on the job.
But I have to carry my head in as if it were a set of jewels.
Eyes, of course, teeth, the cheekbones of appearance, the
    jawbone of discussion.
Others judge me by the resolve with which I continue
    to speak.

3. Gloss of the Poem "Of Salome"

They say to eat your peas or the children will starve in Somalia and Sudan. Europe after the War reclaimed the booty of a million acres. So what are you going to do with the garbage after you separate the edibles from the cans? How's that for a cul-de-sac? You think if you're kind to the old lady no one speaks to it will lead to plenty for everyone—if the world doesn't blow itself up. Change one sensibility at a time. Otherwise, it's one coup d'état after another and the heads clogging the drains. The life force of a child doesn't know the depth of its hunger. A world of playing fields from Eton to Sydney. Meanwhile, Salome is still in charge, the one we die for, as Helen sent forth ships to slaughter the sea. Everyone driving to and from work at the same time because she says to. Backed up at the turn where the homeless camp in sight of a liquor store, their rain-streaked stories written sumi-e style by Magic Markers, telling of military service, lost leases, the crippling turns of fate visible in retreating eyes. While the old man waves at each car and says "God bless you," which he knows has already happened to those who drive past. The numbers don't come out right. I have been repeatedly astonished by the angelic dispositions of people working for the poor, the maimed and the doomed in the most hideous of circumstances where the children die in their care. Salome is the power to change the world, if it comes to that. But you've got to drink your milk or you won't grow strong. Every childhood game and parental admonition leads you to that moment when you change your mind about who is in charge.

4. Ars Poetica at the Window

The history of this moment lengthens in shadow.
Trying to see the past, the light from a lamp is sucked up.
Leaving one in a field of static with a little music in the
    background.
This isn't hard to fathom after midnight.
There are whole sections of the brain without road traffic.
Domains where the mind is but a knapsack.
One needed little things, toiletries and the like, in the
    countryside.
The swirling of the river should have told us.
That whatever tries to move in a straight line shall be
    forced aside.
Shall be bent at every turn, creating a continuous arc.
And so that arcing shall draw a spiral, as it must.
This is clear after midnight, when striving shrivels.
I crave an intimacy too private to speak of.
Truly, one must close one's eyes to see.
True today, true tomorrow, true in the posthumous present.

5. Watercolor on a Book Jacket: Art about Art

Buoyant to look upon this illustration.
The smeared red boat at shore's edge drawn across the lake,
placed there, perhaps, simply by dragging an inked thumb.
The far mountains layered in ruby and tan.
And the bunchy tree casting a moist shadow.
What would you give to be here? This is peace or
an illustration of peace. Distant peasant figures carry their dense
packages as they fade into the mist. The road home is long.
Here there is no life after the flood of news.
The day has been assassinated by those waiting to be born.
It is thus so, always so. We who are old cannot return
        to childhood,
unreal gathering of the flock before shearing.
So we must go back to these pictures of times before we came
        to be.
So that the world may be smeared with birthing,
always with the fresh pigment of life beneath the surface,
and where the imagination may see in an illustration
its future not yet lived. This being the cover of a book,
there is no back to the picture and no passage of time.

6. On the Insularity of the Aesthetic Experience: The Useless Umbrella

Today we will find our art hand- and wind-tossed.
Outdoors, face up, in the rain.
Gray wash over a busted umbrella, red, by the road.
Because the world is possible, our choices are limitless.
A modern angst boot sole and spur, glossy toe and high heel.
Or say just heel and toe, there being just cause.
Just because is sufficient reason for the rain despite knowing.
News of ascendancy seen at the top of a tree in a storm.
Say an island tree, swaying at the edge of the wind.
And woods with spaces a boy might build a fort within.
Our philosophers switched on a lamp to study the dark.
Now he does the same but does not turn on the lamp.
Feeling for honesty sans the famous lantern.
Going upstairs at the celebrated moment without a sense
      of down.
Picture the umbrella, all ways at once.
Then inside-out in the wind, a new way of all together.
A parachute, a hot-air balloon, a sail receiving the wind.
And just as quickly done with, crushed parabola in the weeds.
The pleasing carcass of a purpose flung overboard.
Ballast from a gale made of sense and nonsense.

7. Of the Film *Dancer in the Dark:*
On the Relation of Empathy to Beauty

I told them it was powerful, don't go.
I told them it was much more than they imagined.
I told them the protagonist was put to death, step by step.
Told them they didn't want to see it.
Told them the music would never sing again.
Told them the reviews left something out, something awful.
Told them they would never again sanction executions.
Told them hanging was the worst.
Told them the head, hooded, still looks like a head.
Told them the whole body streaks your eyeballs as it falls.
Told them they would have nightmares.
Told them not to go, not to look, not to let it affect them.
What was I thinking when I told them that?
Go tell them, I thought, because they are my friends.
Like a parent, I wanted to save them from pain.
But the root of all evil is the inability to feel another's pain.
What are we to do as parents?
Are my children merely balls in four-color fragments?
Told them what I thought was everything there was to tell.
Told them it was a beautiful film, but don't go.
Told them not to tell me about it.

8. The Unheard Song

He has taken ether and peyote, but he cannot hear the song.
He has clothed himself in smoke, he has rubbed himself
    with ashes.
Still the leaves dance to the song at the cap ends of their
    branches.
He sees this and believes in a song he cannot hear.
Well, I went out to walk on the moon and there it was.
I had to step over the curb and into the street, but there it was.
The moon lay on the pavement where it had landed in the dark.
I was happy in the asylum that is the night outdoors.
I was there for the stratosphere, and for home.
My purpose in life had been to look out the window.
How free I was behind the well-caulked double panes.
Then the moon lit a path in the dark without exposing me.
I brought it the news and laid it down and ground it out with
    my heel.
I walked all over the moon looking for the famous artifacts.
I stayed outside in the night with nothing else to do.
I knew the spheres were singing on both sides of me.

9. The Case for the Posthumous Present

Fat twists down a rope like suet at the flaming end of the world.
There must have been someone here.
If not, who hung the rope, who made the noose, who climbed?
I was a teacher and could have said I knew but didn't.
Some of my colleagues knew everything, but I knew nothing.
I see now that even a strand of friendship was out of the
     question.
My early teachers thought Jews were cute, they liked it when
     I listened.
The years of need, the straw laundry basket, the hesitation of
     a wheel.
One can picture it in the past or look at it before its time.
I found that I was at home in the future, not in the present.
The proof of my having been born too soon arrived at
     water's edge.
Like many, I never went home for the night without a stop at
     the bay.
To see that it was there, to watch it shift its ponderous weight.
I heard it rumble into melody as it came to shore or ran away.
I heard the intervals of sea wrack tumbling through the tune.
The moon, then, was the cache of our romance.
It held us together as we hung from it, universal locals with
     high hopes.
How earthly the convenience of time and how great was
     our joy.
There was something there, beyond the quick.
More than just alive, we were possible.

10. Coda:

Sounds of the Resurrected Dead Man's Footsteps (Abandonment of Distinctions)

When there is no good or bad, no useful or useless, no up,
no down, no right way, no perfection, then okay it's not
necessary that there be direction: up is down.

When there is no pain, no welcoming, no hospitality, no
disdain, there's no need to be stoical, the opportunity
itself becomes disingenuous, emotion embodied in all
things earth air fire and water.

When there is no adversity, no rise and fall, no ascension,
no decline, no frost too early, no season too soon, then
there's no planet too unstable, no ship in the sky better
than another for the journey of a lifetime.

When there is no attachment, no necessity, no need, no
outcome, no consequence of importance, then naturally
sick is well, and the end leads to a green beginning.

When there is no one face, no two faces, no fragility of
disposition, no anticipation, no revelation at midnight,
then naturally years pass without anyone guessing the
identity of the dead man.

When there is no balance, no even or uneven, no regulation,
no permissible range, no parallax, no one sunrise, then
naturally the dead man from a little salt on his tongue
may concoct a new perspective.

When there is no more luck, no far side to a hard edge, no
final rain, no fatal dehydration, no unwelcome visitation,
no lingering suspicion, no terminal judgment, then the
dead man is all black cats and rabbit paws.

When there is nowhere to go to find him, no circumstance,
no situation, no jewel in the crown, no gem of the ocean,
no pearl of the Antilles, no map, no buried treasure, only
woods and more woods, then suddenly he will appear to
you with a cortege of wolves or foxes in the midst of
your blues.

When there is no measure of candlepower sufficient to
enlighten, no temperature, no tolerance, no voltage, no
current, no draw, no output, then it's historical lunacy to
throw off a moon.

When there is no beginning, no end in sight, no perspective,
no proportion, no discrete color, no golden triangle, no
light at tunnel's end, no subjective complexion, then okay
it's not a matter of where.

When there is no sin, no vice, no turning back, no other way,
no help, no consolation, no punishment, no reward, then
okay there's no good reason, and the ragamuffin arrives
with the royalty.

When there is no more accidental, no inadvertence, no
anthropological terrain sufficiently confined, no chaos
unlinked to further chaos, no anarchy within anarchy, no
thing of discrete substance, then nothing may come
between thought and feeling.

When there is no birthday, no anniversary, no jubilee, no
spree, no holiday, no one mass, meeting or service, then
naturally it is up to each person whether to go ahead or
turn back.

When there is no more wrinkling and weeping, no
physiognomy of pleasure, no anticipation, no abundance,
nothing extra, then okay it's the way it is, not the way we
remember.

When there is no more regularity, no bottle of seeds, no
　　injection of pollen, no gauze to map the outpouring, no
　　tourniquet to stanch the expression, no crutch, no illness
　　or health, then okay why not truth and beauty, why not
　　blameless, helpless truth and beauty?

When there is no end result, no picaresque interval, no
　　immediate or impending, nothing imminent that is not
　　also the past, then why not roses and rubles, peace and
　　prosperity, and okay it's not inconsequential to have come
　　and gone.

When there is no more appetite, no inhalation, no absorption,
　　no osmosis, no digestion, then okay let the reverie
　　commence in the ether.

When there is no one body, no two bodies, no bird that was
　　not a fish, no fish that will not hover, no snake that
　　cannot learn to walk, no man or woman who did not
　　crawl, then the possible and the probable conjoin to
　　grant the blue heron a step.

When there is no more approbation, no license, no all-time
　　immunity, no obedience or disregard, no loyalty that is
　　not also the pick of the litter, no luck but dumb luck,
　　then okay it's not a show, and spunk is what it takes.

When there is nothing but the client's good suit, the jury's
　　self-doubt, the time since the crime, the charts and
　　photos, the measurements and samples, then what
　　knowledge is on trial, what rote redundancy passes for
　　fact, what past lingers?

Where there is no more overriding impulse, no search for the truth that is not a battle to the death, no word left to meaning, no uncontested jurisdiction, no unacceptable flimflam, how then is a spin-off, a by-product, an effect less significant than its cause?

When there is no more this way and that, hither and yon, north and south, no front-and-back, no side-to-side, no kitty-corner, no abreast, no opposite, then suffice it to say that something happened.

When there is no more sacred or heretical, no promise, no guarantee, no warrant that places the millennium, no voltage too high or current too strong, then naturally there can be no one side, no one alone, no other and no otherwise.

When there is no more beseeching or gratitude, no seats remaining on the metaphysical seesaw, no zero-sum activity, no acquisition that is not also a loss, no finitude, then of course the dead man smiles as he blows a kiss through the wispy curtain of closure.

ABOUT THE AUTHOR

Marvin Bell's writing has been part of the conversation for forty years. Flannery O'Connor Professor of Letters at the Writers' Workshop at the University of Iowa and the state of Iowa's first Poet Laureate, he also leads an annual Urban Teachers Workshop for America SCORES, reads and lectures widely, collaborates with composers, musicians and dancers, and teaches a master class for the Rainier Writing Workshop MFA@PLU. He is the creator of the "Dead Man" poems and the "Dead Man Resurrected" poems. His Copper Canyon Press collections include *Iris of Creation*, *The Book of the Dead Man*, *Ardor* (*The Book of the Dead Man, Vol. 2*) and *Nightworks: Poems 1962–2000*. He and his wife, Dorothy, have two sons, Nathan and Jason, who reside, respectively, in Signal Mountain, Tennessee, and New York City.

*Copper Canyon Press wishes to acknowledge the support of
Lannan Foundation in funding the publication and distribution
of exceptional literary works.*

LANNAN LITERARY SELECTIONS 2004

Marvin Bell, *Rampant*
Cyrus Cassells, *More Than Peace and Cypresses*
Ben Lerner, *The Lichtenberg Figures*
Joseph Stroud, *Country of Light*
Eleanor Rand Wilner, *The Girl with Bees in Her Hair*

LANNAN LITERARY SELECTIONS 2000–2003

John Balaban, *Spring Essence: The Poetry of Hồ Xuân Hương*

Hayden Carruth, *Doctor Jazz*

Norman Dubie, *The Mercy Seat: Collected & New Poems, 1967–2001*

Sascha Feinstein, *Misterioso*

James Galvin, *X: Poems*

Jim Harrison, *The Shape of the Journey: New and Collected Poems*

Maxine Kumin, *Always Beginning: Essays on a Life in Poetry*

Antonio Machado, *Border of a Dream: Selected Poems*, translated by Willis Barnstone

W.S. Merwin, *The First Four Books of Poems*

Cesare Pavese, *Disaffections: Complete Poems 1930–1950*, translated by Geoffrey Brock

Antonio Porchia, *Voices*, translated by W.S. Merwin

Kenneth Rexroth, *The Complete Poems of Kenneth Rexroth*, edited by Sam Hamill and Bradford Morrow

Alberto Ríos, *The Smallest Muscle in the Human Body*

Theodore Roethke, *On Poetry & Craft*

Ann Stanford, *Holding Our Own: The Selected Poems of Ann Stanford*, edited by Maxine Scates and David Trinidad

Ruth Stone, *In the Next Galaxy*

Rabindranath Tagore, *The Lover of God*, translated by Tony K. Stewart and Chase Twichell

Reversible Monuments: Contemporary Mexican Poetry, edited by Mónica de la Torre and Michael Wiegers

César Vallejo, *The Black Heralds*, translated by Rebecca Seiferle

C.D. Wright, *Steal Away: Selected and New Poems*

For more on the Lannan Literary Selections, visit:
www.coppercanyonpress.org

The Chinese character for poetry is made up of two parts: "word" and "temple." It also serves as pressmark for Copper Canyon Press.

Founded in 1972, Copper Canyon Press remains dedicated to publishing poetry exclusively, from Nobel laureates to new and emerging authors. The Press thrives with the generous patronage of readers, writers, booksellers, librarians, teachers, students, and funders—everyone who shares the conviction that poetry invigorates the language and sharpens our appreciation of the world.

THE ALLEN FOUNDATION *for* THE ARTS

NATIONAL
ENDOWMENT
FOR THE ARTS

PUBLISHERS' CIRCLE
The Allen Foundation for The Arts
Lannan Foundation
National Endowment for the Arts

EDITORS' CIRCLE
The Breneman Jaech Foundation
Cynthia Hartwig and Tom Booster
Washington State Arts Commission

For information and catalogs:
COPPER CANYON PRESS
Post Office Box 271
Port Townsend, Washington 98368
360/385-4925
www.coppercanyonpress.org